W9-BRT-280

BLUE BANNER BIOGRAPHY

Kevin DURANT

John Bankston

Mitchell Lane
PUBLISHERS

P.O. Box 196
Hockessin, Delaware 19707
Visit us on the web: www.mitchelllane.com
Comments? Email us: mitchelllane@mitchelllane.com

Mitchell Lane
PUBLISHERS

Printing   2   3   4   5   6   7   8   9

Blue Banner Biographies

Abby Wambach	Ice Cube	Miguel Tejada
Adele	Ja Rule	Mike Trout
Alicia Keys	Jamie Foxx	Nancy Pelosi
Allen Iverson	Jay-Z	Natasha Bedingfield
Ashanti	Jennifer Hudson	Nicki Minaj
Ashlee Simpson	Jennifer Lopez	One Direction
Ashton Kutcher	Jessica Simpson	Orianthi
Avril Lavigne	J. K. Rowling	Orlando Bloom
Blake Lively	John Legend	P. Diddy
Bow Wow	Justin Berfield	Peyton Manning
Brett Favre	Justin Timberlake	Prince William
Britney Spears	Kanye West	Queen Latifah
Bruno Mars	Kate Hudson	Robert Downey Jr.
CC Sabathia	Katy Perry	Ron Howard
Carrie Underwood	Keith Urban	Sean Kingston
Chris Brown	Kelly Clarkson	Shakira
Chris Daughtry	Kenny Chesney	Shia LaBeouf
Christina Aguilera	Ke$ha	Shontelle Layne
Clay Aiken	**Kevin Durant**	Soulja Boy Tell 'Em
Cole Hamels	Kristen Stewart	Stephenie Meyer
Condoleezza Rice	Lady Gaga	Taylor Swift
Corbin Bleu	Lance Armstrong	T.I.
Daniel Radcliffe	Leona Lewis	Timbaland
David Ortiz	Lionel Messi	Tim McGraw
David Wright	Lindsay Lohan	Tim Tebow
Derek Jeter	LL Cool J	Toby Keith
Drew Brees	Ludacris	Usher
Eminem	Mariah Carey	Vanessa Anne Hudgens
Eve	Mario	Will.i.am
Fergie	Mary J. Blige	Zac Efron
Flo Rida	Mary-Kate and Ashley Olsen	
Gwen Stefani	Megan Fox	

Library of Congress Cataloging-in-Publication Data applied for.
Bankston, John, 1974–
Kevin Durant / by John Bankston.
     pages cm. — (Blue banner biographies)
Includes bibliographical references and index.
ISBN 978-1-61228-463-7 (library bound)
1. Durant, Kevin, 1984– —Juvenile literature. 2. Baketball players—United States—Biography—Juvenile literature. 3. African American basketball players—Biography—Juvenile literature. I. Title.
GV884.D868B36 2014
796.323092—dc23
[B]
                                                                                    2013023037
eBook ISBN: 9781612285207

ABOUT THE AUTHOR: Born in Boston, Massachusetts, John Bankston began writing articles while still a teenager. Since then, over 200 of his articles have been published in magazines and newspapers across the country, including travel articles in *The Tallahassee Democrat*, *The Orlando Sentinel*, and *The Tallahassean*. He is the author of over 60 biographies for young adults, including Alexander the Great, scientist Stephen Hawking, author F. Scott Fitzgerald, and actor Jodi Foster. A fan of the Celtics growing up, he shares Kevin Durant's admiration for Larry Bird.

PUBLISHER'S NOTE: The following story has been thoroughly researched, and to the best of our knowledge represents a true story. While every possible effort has been made to ensure accuracy, the publisher will not assume liability for damages caused by inaccuracies in the data and makes no warranty on the accuracy of the information contained herein. This story has not been authorized or endorsed by Kevin Durant.

Blue Banner Biography

One and Done

Kevin Durant's team was losing. It was March 4, 2006, and Kevin was playing his last high school basketball game. The stands were packed with over 4,000 screaming fans. All Kevin could do was watch. He'd been benched in the second quarter after picking up his third foul.

Kevin was a small forward for the Montrose Christian School Mustangs, located in Rockville, Maryland. "The small forward should be the best one-on-one player on his team," explains the website ihoops.com. "He needs to be able to have a nose for the basket, and translate that scent into points for his team." Kevin did just that, averaging more than 23 points a game for his team.

The Mustangs' opponent, the Oak Hill Warriors, had won 40 games that season. *USA Today* ranked them the number one high school team in the country. Kevin was very familiar with the team. The year before, he'd been their star player.

Now he was their opponent. Things seemed bleak as Montrose fell behind by 16 points in the fourth quarter. Yet one of Kevin's teammates tipped in a shot at the final buzzer, giving the Mustangs a 74–72 win. "It was one of those games you remember for a long time," Montrose coach Stu Vetter told *Rivals.com*. "We came back and [Kevin] was part of our comeback."

Kevin scored a game-high 31 points. People who saw him play believed he was ready to be a professional basketball player.

Few high school players could match his skills. As a 14-year-old freshman for National Christian Academy—which is located in Fort Washington, Maryland—he was the reason the team drew record numbers of spectators. After the bleachers filled up, fans stood on the auditorium's stage, watching the game as best they could.

By the time Kevin was a senior at Montrose, he was famous from coast to coast. Scout.com ranked him the number-one player in his position. *Parade Magazine* named him a high school basketball All-American, and he earned co-most valuable player honors in the prestigious McDonald's All-American Game. The high-paying, glamorous life of a professional basketball player awaited Kevin. He was very aware of players who went straight from high school to playing pro ball. Like LeBron James, who is now one of the biggest stars in the National Basketball Association (NBA), they became teenage millionaires.

At 18, Kevin Durant was a powerhouse basketball player. Yet he could not follow the same path as James. The rules had changed.

In 2005—the year before Kevin's dramatic final high school basketball game—the NBA and the National Basketball Players Association (NBPA) adopted a new rule. Players had to be 19 and at least one year beyond high school before they could be drafted to play in the NBA. The new rule became known as "one and done." It meant many

On March 29, 2006 Kevin Durant (right) shared Most Valuable Player honors with Chase Budinger during the McDonald's All-American high school basketball game in Encinitas, California. The trophy was presented by coach John Wooden.

high school stars only played college ball for a year before making themselves available for the draft.

Had Kevin graduated in 2005, he almost certainly would have gone straight to the pros. "I think I would have gone this year if I could have," he told the *New York Times* in 2006, "because that's my dream, to go to the NBA. Why not sooner than later?"

Kevin Durant had spent 10 years training to become a professional basketball player. He hoped one more wouldn't make a difference.

Climbing the Hill

*S*uitland-Silver Hill is a predominantly black neighborhood in Prince George's County, Maryland. A short distance from the nation's capital, the region is home to some of the best basketball players in the country. It is also an area beset by violence.

Kevin Wayne Durant was born there on September 29, 1988. He took his mother's last name because at that time Wanda Durant was not married to his father, Wayne Pratt, a police officer at the Library of Congress.

By the time Kevin was eight months old, Pratt was no longer part of the family. Wanda worked at the post office, loading 70-pound bags onto tractor trailers. She worked the night shift, so her mother Barbara Davis watched Kevin and his older brother Tony.

Wanda Durant believed she was working very hard to take care of her family, but after getting passed over for a promotion she realized she might not be working hard enough. "I decided right then my kids would never be in the same situation," she told the *Dallas Morning News* in

2006. "They were always going to work hard to get what they wanted."

At first, Kevin played several sports. When he was 7, he was remembered during a pee wee football practice for allowing the team's weakest player to knock him over. The player had been getting teased and Kevin wanted him to feel better.

> "I hadn't played basketball that much and of course the tallest guy always gets the second look. [Craig] gave me confidence when I didn't have confidence in myself."

When Kevin was 8, his mother enrolled him in the nearby Seat Pleasant Activity Center. He quickly caught the eye of Charles Craig, a large, good-humored man who taught him the basic skills of basketball. "I was a tall skinny kid," Kevin Durant told ESPN's Colleen Dominguez. "I hadn't played basketball that much and of course the tallest guy always gets the second look. [Craig] gave me confidence when I didn't have confidence in myself." He did more for the fatherless boy, taking him to basketball games and movies and providing pocket money. "There were days where I spent the whole day with him," Kevin told Darness Mayberry of *NewsOK*. Craig knew Kevin had potential. He was the first coach to see it. He wouldn't be the last.

During his first year playing basketball, one of Kevin's teammate's grandmothers approached Wanda Durant. She had noticed Kevin's talent and thought he should play for

Taras Brown, the coach of the Prince George's Jaguars. Brown had a reputation for developing top players.

Brown still remembers when he first met Kevin. He was very tall with big feet and flailing arms. Like most players his age, Kevin had only one shot—chucking the ball from his shoulders. Until he was ten, he was a center. In the *Austin American-Statesman*, Brown remembers telling Kevin, "Next summer, you're playing the wing."

It was not long before Kevin realized he only wanted to play basketball. He didn't just want to play for fun. He wanted to make it his career.

This choice came after a basketball tournament in Florida when he was 11. He'd scored 18 points during the second half, helping his team win the championship. Wanda Durant remembered her son coming to her that day and saying, "I want to be a basketball player." As she told *Austin American-Statesman* reporters Kevin Robbins and Mark Rosner, she asked Kevin, "Are you sure?" He said he was. "Then commit to being a basketball player," she told him. "Commit. You think about that. Come back and tell me after you have."

She added, "He did. The next day."

Many preteens dream of a career in professional sports. Wanda Durant and Taras Brown did all they could to help make Kevin's dream come true.

A familiar sight to pro basketball fans: Kevin dunking the ball.

With Brown training him to be a champion, basketball stopped being just fun and games. Sometimes, it started to feel like work. For one thing, Brown told Kevin to stop playing pick-up basketball, five-on-five games that "wouldn't help him develop," as he explained to the *Dallas Morning News.* Instead, Brown says, "I had him working drills all the time."

In every sport, top trainers emphasize the fundamentals—the basics. This is what everyone who plays the sport learns first. It is also the first thing to get sloppy as the fun of games overwhelms technique. After tennis pro Andre Agassi fell from being ranked number-one in the world to 141, he told the Associated Press, "It's been a question of regrouping entirely, getting back to basics and getting back in shape." For Kevin, "regrouping" meant everything from passing drills to working on his shooting while his friends were playing pickup games two courts over. During road trips, Brown would quiz Kevin about plays.

Brown gave Kevin a quote that would become his motto. He told Kevin, "Hard work beats talent when talent fails to work hard."

Brown gave Kevin a quote that would become his motto. He told Kevin, "Hard work beats talent when talent fails to work hard."

When Kevin lost focus or didn't complete a drill, "Hunt's Hill" was waiting. Rising 50 yards (46 meters) and steeper than stadium steps, the L Street hill connected two roads and offered Kevin a connection between hopes and hard reality. At its summit, he could see the Washington, D.C. skyline. Usually he was too tired to take in the vista.

Once when he made a mistake he wound up racing up and down the hill 75 times while his mother waited for him, sitting in her car and reading a book. "I couldn't walk the next day," Kevin admitted to the *Dallas Morning News*.

> *Once when he made a mistake he wound up racing up and down the hill 75 times while his mother waited for him, sitting in her car and reading a book.*

Despite the sheer physical pain of Kevin's ambition, Brown told the *Austin American-Statesman* that "He wouldn't quit. I would give Kevin days off and he'd show up at the rec. He wanted to live in the gym."

The lessons were hard, but the people in Kevin's life believe they prepared him for the challenges ahead. When Kevin was 13, his father returned to the family. He married Wanda, who took his last name, and the family grew. Kevin would have a sister, Brianna, and another brother, Rayvonne.

"My wife did a tremendous job with the boys," Wayne Pratt told the *Dallas Morning News*. "She is the rock and strength of the family." Yet even as Kevin's home life became more stable, his life on the basketball court was anything but.

Escape

By the time Kevin Durant was in the eighth grade he wasn't just taller than his classmates. At 6 feet, 2 inches, he was taller than most of his teachers. His classmates paid less attention to his talents on the courts than to his size-11 feet, which were covered by the used Lisa Leslie or Sheryl Swoopes shoes his mother bought him. "I played well in those," he told ESPN.com. "I hated, hated, hated going to school."

Trevor Brown was the coach of National Christian Academy when he saw Kevin playing for the Jaguars. "These dudes were pros," he told the *Austin American-Statesman* in 2007. "This was eighth grade and these dudes were pros."

He offered Kevin a scholarship to attend the private National Christian Academy. Midway through Kevin's first year, Brown bumped him up to the varsity. Kevin's promotion made the older players angry. They decided they weren't going to pass the ball to the new arrival.

Kevin was furious. He wanted to quit. His mother and Taras Brown wouldn't let him.

They told him to keep playing his best. Eventually things would change. They did. By the end of the year, the Eagles were drawing record crowds. That summer he grew nearly half a foot. As a 6-foot, 8-inch sophomore, Kevin had little trouble convincing the players to give him the ball.

When he was a junior, Kevin transferred to the Oak Hill Academy. The school is in Mouth of Wilson, Virginia, 360 miles from his home. The century-old Baptist boarding school had produced NBA players like Carmelo Anthony, Ron Mercer, and Jerry Stackhouse. Playing in such elite company could provide the final seasoning Kevin needed for college and the pros. Then he received devastating news.

On April 30, 2005, Charles Craig was murdered after breaking up a fight between a friend of his and another man. It was, as Kevin later described it, a case of being in the wrong place at the wrong time. "I thought he was like superman," Kevin told ESPN's Colleen Dominguez. "I didn't think anything would happen to him. To hear that, to hear that he wasn't going to be around anymore—I was shocked."

Kevin didn't know what to do. He felt lost. Yet even in his darkest moments, the man he calls his godfather—Taras Brown—offered sage advice. "I wanted to do something for him [Craig] but I didn't know what," Kevin told ESPN. "My godfather said the best thing you can do for him is wear 35. That's the age he was when he got murdered." Years later, Kevin's number 35 jersey would become one of the NBA's best-selling articles of apparel. Sometimes Kevin sneaks a look into the stands and is thrilled to see fans wearing it. "Without them knowing, they've got a piece of Chuck on," he told Darnell Mayberry of NewsOK.

Kevin Durant acknowledges the cheers of the home crowd after making yet another spectacular play during Game 1 of the Western Conference Semifinals on May 5, 2013 against the Memphis Grizzlies.

Getting Noticed

*A*t first, Kevin Durant was angry. His mentor had been murdered. "On the court, I wasn't letting nobody say nothing to me . . . I'm automatically thinking, 'Oh, I'm better than you,' or 'I'm the best player here,'" he admitted to ESPN.com. Kevin played his rage. He drew more fouls than usual and trash-talked opponents. He told his opponents how many points he'd score on them. He showboated. And for the first time, he failed.

He started missing shots. Suddenly people were saying he was overhyped and too thin to make it in college ball, let alone the NBA. Kevin started to worry that he'd never see his dreams come true.

"And then it popped in my head: it was all the bragging and boasting," he told ESPN.com. "That's not the way to do it. It was a great lesson I was taught by God, man . . . It could have been worse. I could have been injured, basketball could have been taken away from me."

Kevin was blessed, not just with strong talent but also with a strong support system. His parents were together. His former coaches were there for him. Kevin left Oak Hill for Montrose Christian for his senior year. A more humble Kevin Durant broke records and won games. He also made a commitment to play for the college which had first noticed him.

Kevin had been playing for National Christian Academy when University of Texas Longhorns assistant coach Russell Springmann spotted the talented sophomore. Springmann had been scouting another player at the War on the Shore, an invitational tournament in Milford, Delaware. He saw Kevin sink a three-point shot from the corner. "I didn't see much of the game," he told the *Austin American Statesman*. "But that was the one that stood out."

Springmann filled out a Player Profile form on Kevin Durant. It was the first step to being selected to play for the Longhorns.

Although he hoped for a pro career right out of high school, Kevin Durant's athletic development was greatly helped by his year at the University of Texas and Coach Rick Barnes, seen here.

Less than a month after Charles Craig was killed, Kevin headed to Texas for an official recruiting visit. Kevin's father accompanied him. According to the *Austin American-Statesman*, Springmann told Pratt, "The one thing I can promise you is that your son is going to be cared for."

Later that night, Kevin enjoyed a steak dinner with his father, Springmann, and Texas head coach Rick Barnes. When Pratt saw his son laughing with Barnes, he told Springmann that was what he was looking for. Not long after, Kevin signed a letter of intent committing to Texas and enrolled there in the fall of 2006.

Despite his talents, Kevin faced challenges. He was still very thin for college ball—he weighed under 200 pounds his last year of high school. Strength and conditioning coach Todd Wright worked with him. Besides a weight program, Wright tried to change Kevin's eating habits. He pushed him to eat breakfast—a meal he usually skipped—and cut

Despite being a freshman, Kevin Durant started every game. During the season opener against Alcorn State, he scored 20 points for the Texas Longhorns—a new freshman record.

down on the candy and cookies he enjoyed so much. Kevin gained nearly 20 pounds of muscle.

As a high school freshman, Kevin had quickly leaped to varsity play. As a college freshman, he started every game. Kevin scored 20 points against Alcorn State in the season-opening game, which at the time was a freshman record for his school. Kevin scored at least 20 points in 30 different games. Twice he scored 37 points. He averaged over 25 points and 11 rebounds per game. He was named the Division I Player of the Year by the National Association of Basketball Coaches. It was the first time they'd given the award to a freshman.

When the Longhorns lost to the University of Southern California in the second round of the NCAA's March Madness basketball playoffs and their season came to an end, most people expected that Kevin would soon become a professional basketball player. On April 11, 2007, he declared himself eligible for the NBA draft.

Kevin drives toward the hoop against Francisco Garcia #32 of the Houston Rockets during Game Six of the Western Conference Quarterfinals of the 2013 NBA Playoffs.

CHAPTER 5

Thunderstruck

When the NBA Draft began on June 28, 2007, Ohio State's Greg Oden was the number-one choice. He was selected by the Portland Trail Blazers. The Seattle Sonics quickly snapped up Kevin as the second overall pick. He soon realized that the team was being constructed around him. It was a tremendous amount of pressure for a 19-year-old. "I would get guarded by the best guys every night and I had to guard some of the best guys every night," he told ESPN.com.

He spent a fair amount of time on the floor, knocked over by bigger guys. He wasn't eating right, putting away chicken wings and candy. Still, Kevin averaged over 20 points a game. With Oden missing the entire 2007–08 season due to a knee injury, Kevin was named NBA Rookie of the Year. Despite his talents, however, the Sonics only won 20 games while losing 62.

During that season, the Sonics had fought with city officials over the team's arena. In 2008, the team moved to Oklahoma City, Oklahoma. It was a city with a tragic past.

Playing for the Seattle Sonics during an exhibition game against the Golden State Warriors on October 23, 2007, Kevin Durant is knocked to the floor.

Surrounded by the people who made him who he is today—his family—Kevin Durant accepts the Rookie of the Year award in 2008.

On April 19, 1995, Timothy McVeigh parked a rented truck in front of the Alfred P. Murrah Federal Building in downtown Oklahoma City. A bomb inside the truck exploded and killed 168 people, including 19 children. McVeigh was executed six years later. He had been responsible for the most deadly act of terrorism within the United States until the attacks of September 11th, 2001.

Many people in Oklahoma City wanted to change the city's tragic image. They improved the downtown and rebuilt the area where the federal building had stood. And they used $120 million in sales-tax revenue to construct an arena. It became the team's new home.

"As a judge I deal with evidence," Oklahoma Supreme Court Justice Steven Taylor told ESPN.com. "The NBA team arriving in Oklahoma City was Exhibit A that Oklahoma survived the bombing."

When local residents watched the Thunder's first practice in Oklahoma City, Kevin was mobbed by grateful fans. They proved their gratitude by packing the new arena, even if the team started with a 3–29 record.

Kevin wanted to lead his team to the playoffs. He begged his coach, Scott Brooks, to never take him out of the game. Brooks didn't think Kevin would last for all four quarters. Kevin set out to prove him wrong. He started working out harder and eating breakfast. By the end of the season, the Thunder had improved somewhat and finished 23-59.

In the 2009–10 season, Kevin led the Thunder to the playoffs with a 50–32 record. Although they lost to the Los Angeles Lakers in the first round of the playoffs, people began to realize that Oklahoma actually had a pro basketball team. At 21, Kevin became the youngest player in NBA history to win the scoring title, with an average of 30.1 points per game.

He won the scoring title again in 2010–11 as the Thunder advanced to the Western Conference Finals. They lost to the Dallas Mavericks, who won the NBA championship. In 2012, the Thunder went all the way to the NBA Finals, facing the Miami Heat. The Thunder lost the series, four games to one.

Kevin admitted to the Associated Press that the defeat was painful. "I wanted to win so bad. I wanted to win for the city, I wanted to win for of course our team, myself, I wanted to win for so many people. Man, you kind of feel like you let them down just a little bit."

He didn't have time to brood over the loss. He was a vital member of the U.S. basketball team at the London Olympic Games later that summer. He set a U.S. record for points scored in a single Olympics with 156. That included 30 points in the gold medal win over Spain.

He also added acting to his list of accomplishments, starring in the movie *Thunderstruck*. Kevin played a pro basketball player who switches abilities with a klutzy 16-year-old fan. "Durant's personal motto, which is repeated often, is 'Hard work beats talent when talent fails to work hard,'" said *Washington Post* movie critic Sean O'Connell. "And that slogan acts as the backbone of the film, educating young audience members about the importance of practice."

> *Kevin added acting to his list of accomplishments when starring in Thunderstruck. Kevin played a pro basketball player who switches abilities with a klutzy 16-year-old fan.*

Thunder fans looked forward to the 2012–13 season, and the team rewarded them with a 60–22 regular season record, the best in the NBA's Western Conference. But an injury to Russell Westbrook, one of the team's best players, was a factor in the Thunder's second-round elimination by the Memphis Grizzlies, four games to one.

Basketball soon took a back seat to the forces of nature. On May 20, a vicious tornado ripped through Moore, a suburb of Oklahoma City. It killed 23 people, including several children. Kevin immediately stepped up, pledging $1 million to help victims of the disaster. "As the day went on and I saw the footage and the casualties and the houses being blown away, it was tough to

Kevin Durant scores another three-point shot over Simas Jasaitis #10 of Lithuania during the Men's Basketball Preliminary Round match at the London 2012 Olympic Games on August 4, 2012 in London, England.

see," Kevin told the Associated Press. "I call Oklahoma City my home. I go through Moore all the time. It's unfortunate. We're going to come together as a city like we always do and we're going to bounce back."

That was just the start. Kevin toured Moore, giving autographs and encouraging words to victims of the damage. He raised several million dollars from the Thunder, a combination of the NBA and NBPA, Nike, and other sources. "That he continues to use his stature and relationships to continue to make massive contributions to an effort that's going to take an awful lot of time, money and commitment is just remarkable; it's like every time you think Durant's maxed out the degree to which he seems too good to be true, he reaches another level," said sports blogger Dan Devine. "Oklahoma City's pretty lucky to have this dude as part of the community."

> *"I call Oklahoma City my home. I go through Moore all the time. It's unfortunate. We're going to come together as a city like we always do and we're going to bounce back."*

On July 26, 2013, Kevin became engaged to Monica Wright, a guard for the Minnesota Lynx of the Women's National Basketball Association. They first met at the McDonald's All-American Game in 2006.

Despite all of Kevin's achievements (and an estimated $30 million dollars in annual earnings) Thunder head coach Brooks told *USA Today*, "He treats everybody like they're the most important person he's met. That is not picking and choosing those moments. He does it every time."

1988   Kevin Wayne Durant is born on September 29th to Wayne Pratt and Wanda Durant.

1996   Begins playing for the PG Jaguars in Prince George's County, Maryland; the team's coach, Taras Brown, works with Kevin on fundamentals.

2002   Enters National Christian Academy in Fort Washington, Maryland.

2004   Enrolls in the Oak Hill Academy, a private boarding school in Mouth of Wilson, Virginia.

2005   Plays for Montrose Christian School; commits to playing for the University of Texas Longhorns.

2006   Begins playing for the University of Texas Longhorns.

2007   Is named the College Player of the Year; is drafted by the Seattle Sonics

2008   Is named Rookie of the Year by the NBA; the Seattle Sonics move to Oklahoma City and are renamed the Thunder.

2009   Leads the Thunder in scoring during the team's inaugural season in Oklahoma City.

2010   The Thunder reach the first round of the NBA Playoffs; Kevin leads the league in scoring.

2011   The Thunder reach the Western Conference Finals.

2012   The Thunder make it to the NBA Finals; Kevin sets U.S. scoring record in the Olympics as Team USA wins the gold medal.

2013   Kevin donates $1 million to help victims of a tornado that devastates Moore, Oklahoma; announces engagement to basketball player Monica Wright.

2014   Wins awards for Best Male Athlete of Year and Best NBA Player.

Regular Season Stats

Season	Team	G	RPG	APG	SPG	TO	PPG
2007-08	SEA	80	4.4	2.4	1.0	2.9	20.3
2008-09	OKC	74	6.5	2.8	1.3	3.0	25.3
2009-10	OKC	82	7.6	2.8	1.4	3.3	30.1
2010-11	OKC	78	6.8	2.7	1.1	2.8	27.7
2011-12	OKC	66	8.0	3.5	1.3	3.8	28.0
2012-13	OKC	81	7.9	4.6	1.4	3.5	28.1
2013-14	OKC	81	7.4	5.5	1.3	3.5	32.0
Career		542	6.9	3.5	1.3	3.2	27.4

Playoff Stats

Season	Team	G	RPG	APG	SPG	TO	PPG
2009-10	OKC	6	7.7	2.3	0.5	3.7	25.0
2010-11	OKC	17	8.2	2.8	0.9	2.5	28.6
2011-12	OKC	20	7.4	3.7	1.5	3.2	28.5
2012-13	OKC	11	9.0	6.3	1.3	3.9	30.8
2013-14	OKC	19	8.9	3.9	1.0	3.8	29.6
Career		73	8.2	3.8	1.1	3.3	28.9

(SEA=Seattle Sonics, OKC=Oklahoma City Thunder, G=Games, RPG=Rebounds per game, APG= Assists per game, SPG=Steals per game, TO=Turnovers per game, PPG=Points per game)

FURTHER READING

Further Reading

Doeden, Matt. *Kevin Durant: Basketball Superstar*. Mankato, MN: Capstone Press, 2012.

Gitlin, Marty. *Kevin Durant: NBA Superstar*. Minneapolis: ABDO Publishing, 2013.

Sandler, Michael and Charlie Zegers, *Kevin Durant*. New York: Bearport Publishing, 2012.

Sandler, Jeff. *Kevin Durant*. Minneapolis: Lerner Publications, 2012.

Works Consulted

Broadcast Interview

"In the Spotlight," Interview by Colleen Dominguez. ESPN. http://www.youtube.com/watch?v=gQZahU_1cQo

Periodicals

_____. "Durant Puts Basketball First and Second," the *New York Times*, June 27, 2007. http://www.nytimes.com/2007/06/27/sports/basketball/27durant.html?_r=0

Barr, Josh "The King of the Hill," the *Washington Post*. March 5, 2006. http://www.washingtonpost.com/wp-dyn/content/article/2006/03/04/AR2006030401331.html

Beck, Howard. "N.B.A. Draft Will Close Book on High School Stars," the *New York Times*. June 28, 2005. http://www.nytimes.com/2005/06/28/sports/basketball/28draft.html?_r=0.

Brown, Chip. "UT's Durant: Righteous Talent," the *Dallas Morning News*, November 8, 2006. http://web.archive.org/web/20070926224909/http://www.texassports.com/doc_lib/newsstand_mbb/DMN-UTs_Durant_rightous_talent.pdf.

"Finals Pain Remains for Kevin Durant," Associated Press. July10, 2012. http://espn.go.com/espn/print?id=8154684&type=story.

Jenkins, Lee. "The Iceman Cometh," *Sports Illustrated*, June 25, 2012. http://sportsillustrated.cnn.com/vault/article/magazine/MAG1200948/index.htm

Krawczynski, Jon. "Thunder star Kevin Durant makes $1M tornado pledge," The Associated Press, May 21, 2013. http://sports.yahoo.com/news/thunder-star-kevin-durant-makes-165309505--nba.html

Mayberry, Darnell. "Why 35? The story behind a jersey number and Kevin Durant's devotion to his coach." NewsOK, March 24, 2010. http://newsok.com/why-35-the-story-behind-a-jersey-number-and-kevin-durants-devotion-to-his-coach/article/3448737

O'Donnell, Sean. "The NBA's own 'Freaky Friday.'" *Washington Post*, August 24, 2012. http://www.washingtonpost.com/gog/movies/thunderstruck,1097529/critic-review.html

Patrick, Dan. "Just My Type," *Sports Illustrated*, March 12, 2012. http://sportsillustrated.cnn.com/vault/article/magazine/MAG1195693/index.htm

Peterson, Anne. "Agassi tops Sampras to Win Title," Associated Press, February 16, 1998. http://www.reviewjournal.com/lvrj_home/1998/Feb-16-Mon-1998/sports/6965252.html

Robbins, Kevin and Mark Rosner. "The Making of Kevin Durant," *Austin American-Statesman*. February 28, 2007. http://grfx.cstv.com/schools/tex/graphics/newsstand/ns_030107_durant.pdf

Thomsen, Ian. "Let the Rivalry Begin," *Sports Illustrated*, June 18, 2012. http://sportsillustrated.cnn.com/vault/article/magazine/MAG1200402/index.htm

On the Internet

"Kevin Durant," Scouthoops.Scout.com. http://scouthoops.scout.com/a.z?s=75&p=8&c=1&nid=1111705

Devine, Dan. "Kevin Durant taps Nike to donate $1M in products, sneaker profits to Oklahoma tornado relief." Ball Don't Lie, Yahoo.com, May 24, 2013. http://sports.yahoo.com/blogs/nba-ball-dont-lie/kevin-durant-taps-nike-donate-1-million-products-145141563.html

Picker, David. "In the NBA's Age Game, Colleges Are Big Winners." The New York Times, April 22, 2006. http://www.nytimes.com/2006/04/22/sports/22jordan.html

Tayyar, Paul. "The Small Forward's Responsibilities," iHoops.com.
    http://www.ihoops.com/training-room/coaches/the-small-
    forwards-responsibilities.htm
"Terror Hits Home: The Oklahoma City Building," FBI.gov.
    http://www.fbi.gov/about-us/history/famous-cases/
    oklahoma-city-bombing
The Official Home of Kevin Durant
    http://kevindurant35.com
The Official Youth Basketball Website of USA Basketball
    www.ihoops.com
Kevin Durant Stats, Bio and Game Logs
    http://www.nba.com/playerfile/kevin_durant/index.html

INDEX